#IChooseME

Journal

Dare2LoveYou.com

All rights reserved. No part of this publication may be produced, distributed, or transmitted in any form or by any means, including photocopying, recording, or other electronic or mechanical methods, without the prior written permission of the publisher, except in the case of brief quotations embodied in critical reviews and certain other noncommercial uses permitted by copyright law. All pictures are held by commercial license and may not be duplicated by anyone without the express permission. For permission requests, write to the publisher, at Attention: Permissions Coordinator, tiffany@tiffanydkelly.com

ISBN:

Please note that we have made every effort to ensure accuracy of information presented in this planner was correct at press time, the author and publisher do not assume and hereby disclaim any liability to any party for any loss, damage, or disruption caused by errors or omissions, whether such errors or omissions result from negligence, accident, or any other cause. Results commensurate with application and implementation. No guarantees of personal success. As with all information, your success is dependent upon many factors, including you. Results not guaranteed.

Tiffany D. Kelly Consulting 2020 © All Rights Reserved. Duplication Not Permitted.

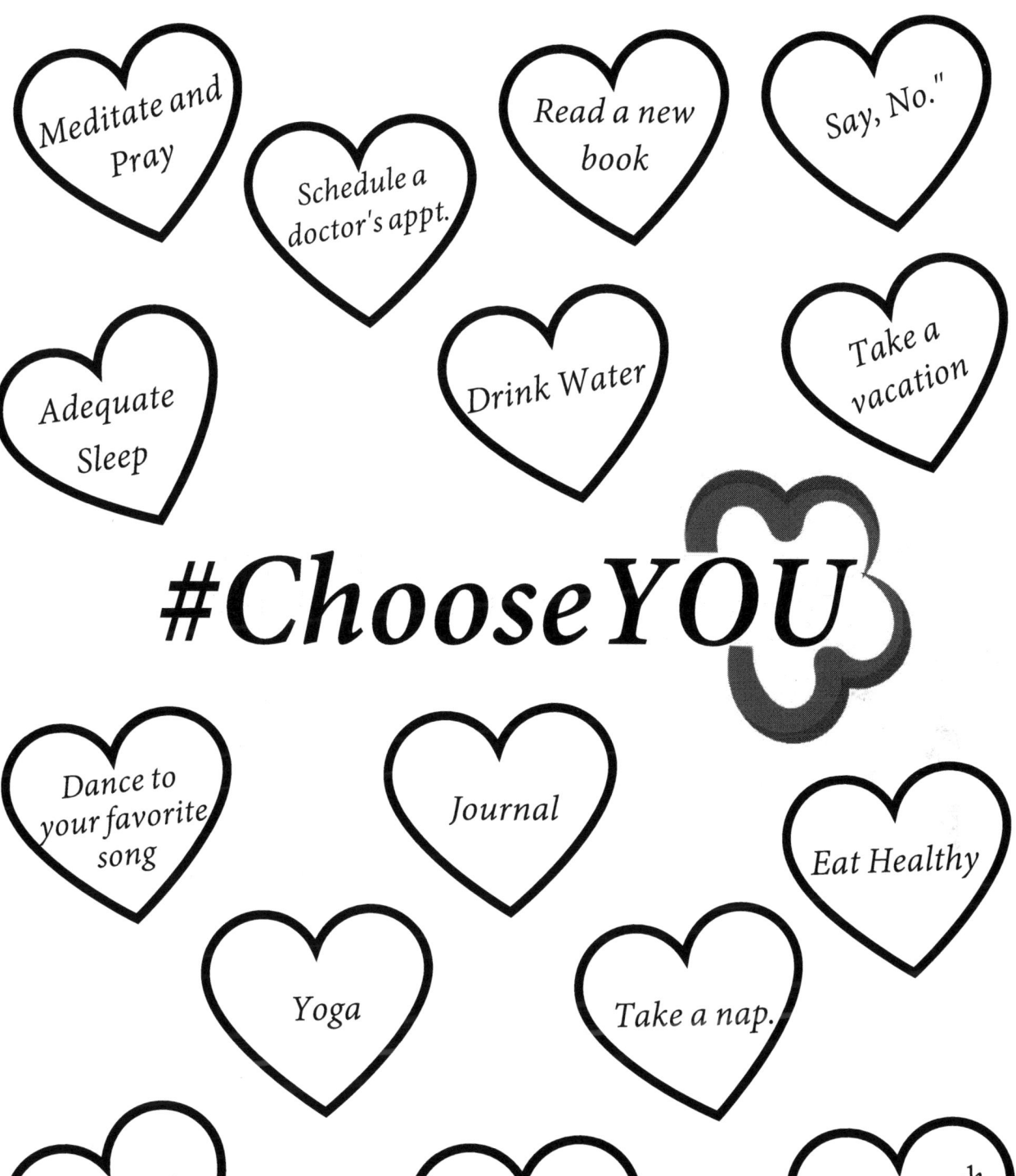

- Meditate and Pray
- Schedule a doctor's appt.
- Read a new book
- Say, No."
- Adequate Sleep
- Drink Water
- Take a vacation

#ChooseYOU

- Dance to your favorite song
- Journal
- Eat Healthy
- Yoga
- Take a nap.
- Go for a Walk
- Take a fitness class
- Have lunch w/a friend

Choose YOU today and every day!

Choose YOU today and every day!

Choose YOU today and every day!

Choose YOU today and every day!

Choose YOU today and every day!

Choose YOU today and every day!

Choose YOU today and every day!

Choose YOU today and every day!

Choose YOU today and every day!

Choose YOU today and every day!

Choose YOU today and every day!

Choose YOU today and every day!

Choose YOU today and every day!

Choose YOU today and every day!

Choose YOU today and every day!

Choose YOU today and every day!

Choose YOU today and every day!

Choose YOU today and every day!

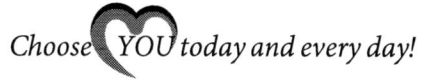

Choose YOU today and every day!

Choose YOU today and every day!

Choose YOU today and every day!

Choose YOU today and every day!

Choose YOU today and every day!

Choose YOU today and every day!

Choose YOU today and every day!

Choose YOU today and every day!

Choose YOU today and every day!

Choose YOU today and every day!

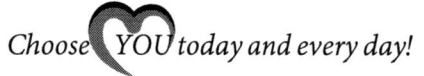

Choose YOU today and every day!

Choose YOU today and every day!

Choose YOU today and every day!

Choose YOU today and every day!

Choose YOU today and every day!

Choose YOU today and every day!

Choose YOU today and every day!

Choose YOU today and every day!

Choose YOU today and every day!

Choose YOU today and every day!

Choose YOU today and every day!

Choose YOU today and every day!

Choose YOU today and every day!

Choose YOU today and every day!

Choose YOU today and every day!

Choose YOU today and every day!

Choose YOU today and every day!

Choose YOU today and every day!

Choose YOU today and every day!

Choose YOU today and every day!

Choose YOU today and every day!

Choose YOU today and every day!

Choose YOU today and every day!

Choose YOU today and every day!

Choose YOU today and every day!

Choose YOU today and every day!

Choose YOU today and every day!

Choose YOU *today and every day!*

Choose YOU today and every day!

Choose YOU today and every day!

Choose YOU today and every day!

Choose YOU today and every day!

Choose YOU today and every day!

Choose YOU today and every day!

Choose YOU today and every day!

Choose YOU today and every day!

Choose YOU today and every day!

Choose YOU today and every day!

Choose YOU today and every day!

Choose YOU today and every day!

Choose YOU today and every day!

Choose YOU today and every day!

Choose YOU today and every day!

Choose YOU today and every day!

Choose YOU today and every day!

Choose YOU today and every day!

Choose YOU today and every day!

Choose YOU today and every day!

Choose YOU today and every day!

Choose YOU today and every day!

Choose YOU today and every day!

Choose YOU today and every day!

Choose YOU today and every day!

Choose YOU today and every day!

Choose YOU today and every day!

Choose YOU today and every day!

Choose YOU today and every day!

Choose YOU today and every day!

Choose YOU today and every day!

Choose YOU today and every day!

Choose YOU today and every day!

Choose YOU today and every day!

Choose YOU today and every day!

Choose YOU today and every day!

Choose YOU today and every day!

Choose YOU today and every day!

Choose YOU today and every day!

Choose YOU today and every day!

Choose YOU today and every day!

Choose YOU today and every day!

Choose YOU today and every day!

Choose YOU today and every day!

Choose YOU today and every day!

Choose YOU today and every day!

Choose YOU today and every day!

Choose YOU today and every day!

Choose YOU today and every day!

Choose YOU today and every day!

Choose YOU today and every day!

Choose YOU today and every day!

Choose YOU today and every day!

Choose YOU today and every day!

Choose YOU today and every day!

Choose YOU today and every day!

Choose YOU today and every day!

Choose YOU today and every day!

Choose YOU today and every day!

Choose YOU today and every day!

Choose YOU today and every day!

Choose YOU today and every day!

Choose YOU today and every day!

Choose YOU today and every day!

Choose YOU today and every day!

Choose YOU today and every day!

Choose YOU today and every day!

Choose YOU today and every day!

Choose YOU today and every day!

Choose YOU today and every day!

Choose YOU today and every day!

Choose YOU today and every day!

Choose YOU today and every day!

Choose YOU today and every day!

Choose YOU today and every day!

Choose YOU today and every day!

Choose YOU today and every day!

Choose YOU today and every day!

Choose YOU today and every day!

Choose YOU today and every day!

Choose YOU today and every day!

Choose YOU today and every day!

Choose YOU today and every day!

Choose YOU today and every day!

Choose YOU today and every day!

Choose YOU today and every day!

Choose YOU today and every day!

Choose YOU today and every day!

Choose YOU today and every day!

Choose YOU today and every day!

Choose YOU today and every day!

Choose YOU today and every day!

Choose YOU today and every day!

Choose YOU today and every day!

Made in the USA
Columbia, SC
20 February 2023